A ONE chapter book

The LuckyPreneur!

Does This Guy Have a Horseshoe up his Wazoo?

W.T. Hamilton
Your Invincible Power

Copyright © 2018 Your Invincible Power

All rights reserved

Published by W.T. Hamilton

No part of this publication may be reproduced, stored in a retrieval system, or transmitted in any form or by any means, electronic, mechanical, photocopied, rerecorded, scanned, or otherwise, except as permitted under Canadian copyright law, without the prior written permission of the author.

Disclaimer:

While the authors and publisher of this book have made reasonable efforts to ensure the accuracy of the information contained herein, the authors and publisher assume no liability with respect to losses or damage caused, or alleged to be caused, by any reliance on any information contained herein and disclaim any and all warranties, expressed or implied, as to the accuracy or reliability of said information. The authors and publisher make no representations or warranties with respect to the accuracy or completeness of the contents of this work and specifically disclaim all warranties. The advice and strategies contained herein may not be suitable for every situation.

ISBN: 9781720271345
Imprint: Independently published
Published: Sept 12, 2018

Before We Dive into this Awesome Book…

'Welcome to the madness.' Those were the words he thought to himself as he stared at the blank page which would become the intro to his new book series.

'Welcome to the insanity of this journey.' It was this feeling that swelled up inside him with excitement as he began to realize just what he had created. And in that moment of awareness he felt gratitude for just how blessed he was. He knew he was a lucky MoFo.

Luck in hindsight seemed to be his best friend. It was always there for him when he really needed it. He wasn't a *'half glass'* type guy, he was an *'I expect something to always be in the glass'* type guy. So luck followed him because he expected it to follow him. Allowing this to be his safety net enabled him to do what he loved to do the most in life, take risks.

It was in this gambling attitude, this roll the dice lifestyle and in the belief that there will always be *something in the glass* that he was able to do something cool, fun and powerful. Something very few get to do in life. He created the One Chapter book series.

But cool ideas come with many challenges. There are struggles build into every journey that must be lived and experienced before one can move forward. *'Why is life so brutal? Why do I have to go through shit before I can have shit?!?!'* Not the thoughts of a luckupreneur but these were and often are his real life thoughts.

> *'What is the purpose of making it so hard to succeed in anything worth succeeding in? Why is life/success designed in this way?'*

He asked himself these question expecting an answer. The questions would always come after the excitement of the beginning began to fade. After the motivating words of people like Tony Robbins wore off. When what was in the glass was tasted more like a mouthful of sour grapes.

'But how can you teach it if you haven't lived it?' This was the question and the answer that came to him amidst the frustration. The experience was his authenticity. The struggle was his teacher. The journey would give him the cheat sheets to share with others.

'Success is all about breadcrumbs and nuggets. It's about gathering information and applying it to what you're doing now. Customizing it to fit your vision of success!'

Boom! Someone detonated a mind bomb inside him, and it rattled his cranium. This was what he needed to understand the purpose and importance of succeeding at something new and sharing the knowledge. This gave him the drive needed to push past the struggles of the entrepreneurial life. The hurdles of managing resources and balancing creativity with marketing, promoting and engaging, all while trying to build a life outside of business.

'This is not a simple task.' He thought as he considered everything before him.

'But whatever is?' He already knew the answer. Nothing worthwhile. And then he suddenly had the idea, like a piece of wisdom that suddenly slapped him upside his head.

'Write about what you've already lived and mastered. Share those stories while you live your new stories.'

These thoughts would always find him in form of ideas of inspiration. A world wind of rapid creativity would follow until the idea was in complete form. But being a *'There's always something in the glass'* type of guy he realized he had an unfair advantage.

He had a friend named Luck.

The more he thought about it the more he could see how to use this unfair advantage in his business to create what he would fondly call, The LuckPreneur. And this is why he created this chapter in the series. He knew that everyone has this advantage once they learn how to recognize it and utilize it. What once began as a concept soon became a passion and a mission.

As he sat in thought of how he wanted to share his experiences and hurdles he wrote this...

I want to WARN you. You are about to read a book that has been created to do one thing and one thing only. Solve your entrepreneur problem. That is the purpose and ambition of this book.

Now this was not written to simply entertain you although it will. There are also hidden nuggets and Capt'n Obvious ones too, placed not only throughout this book but within the pages of the entire One Chapter Book series.

This series was created to solve the first problem I needed to fix in my journey to become a successful entrepreneur. My journey always led me to time consuming research often from very bland sources to get the answer to the challenge I was facing. I have stacks of ½ read books to prove it.

One day while looking at this very stack I realized just like Frank Costanza did on the fateful day, as he was delivering blows to some guys head, 'There's got to be another way'. Staring at that huge stack of books was my Costanza moment.

This was the birth of the One Chapter Book series. Helping Millennials Solve Entrepreneur Problems One Chapter Book at a time! Yep, that's the slogan, just came up with that bad boy after writing the first four books!

It was in this spirit that a new venture was born. It was a moment of knowing that led him to create something that everyone needed but no one really thought about before. As the entrepreneur mantra goes, business are started by addressing a problem or filling a need.

'Luck is a friend you'll want to have on your side.' He wrote as he sipped his coffee.

'Luck is something you can build into your business.' This was something he had taught and it would become the key to his new book. As he sat thinking of just the ways to write this book the subtitle suddenly became clear and the conversation around it became an image that made him chuckle. But his only question at that point was, *'Is it going too far?'*

He reached into his pocket were he always kept two dice. He held them for a moment for they reminded him of one thing and one thing only. He was a risk taker and it was time to roll the dice!

Who the Phuc is W.T?!?!?

W.T. Hamilton is a mentor, author, coach who is also an expert in the law of attraction. He teaches the law of attraction from the non-spiritual side showing people how to apply it to business and how to create success in their lives.

He has written many motivational and inspirational books with his Mom making them the Unlikely Duo. Now he is expanding his message to utilize his many years of experience in the business world.

He is an entrepreneur who has run his own successful management and sales consulting business and continues to work in that field. He has also expanded into coaching and mentoring other entrepreneurs.

At any given time you'll find him on stage sharing personal stories that will motivate and inspire the audience to see life in all the infinite possibilities as he lives his truths. He had a dream of speaking on stage but in the early days he had a lack of skills to do it until he joined Forest City Toastmasters in London, Ontario Canada where he crafted the skill of entertaining using motivational messages.

Born in Leister England to an English Mother & a Jamaican Father then moving to Canada at the age of four, he has a diverse background that has enabled him to really connect with all types of people. Growing up with a multicultural background allowed him to follow his own rules. He wasn't defined by any one culture so he was able to enjoy many cultures including ones outside of his background.

He became a writer by chance, when learning about the law of attraction he was turned off by all the spirituality attached to it and struggled to connect with it at first. He decided to learn it on his own and started writing about his experience with it as he learned what worked for him and what didn't.

At the same time, his Mom was planning to write a book about her understanding of this universal law. When she found out he had been writing about his experiences with it too their first book – Your Invincible Power: Open the Door to Unlimited Wealth, Health and Joy was born. As was this Unlikely Duo.

His Mom was writing from the spiritual side while he was writing from the practical application. This caused some interesting debates and conversations but it somehow worked and they still work together on many project to this day.

W.T.'s journey has led him to many great accomplishments traveling to different cities to speak, do book signing, coach and enjoy life. He is passionate about sales consulting and success coaching but also loves to follow his creative intuition whenever it prompts him.

He is an explorer, a skeptic at heart, an adventurer and risk taker always looking to push his limits and challenge his skills. Believing the comfort zone is where dreams go to die, he is always looking for new ways to test what he knows and what he can do.

From YouTube Channels that he turned into a podcast style show to launching an iTunes channel on a whim and creating online training courses because it seemed like a good way to reach more people. You never know what he will do next and neither does he.

He has found the way to use the law of attraction and still be authentic to who he is. He has learned how to use it to focus on success and leveling up his life. This has become his core message and his true passion.

To create a way for everyone to use this method of thinking on purpose to achieve the things their most passionate about. To live life with passion and to enjoy what you do every day.

That's who the phuc W.T. is!

Behind the Scenes Info – Part Five

Luck. Oh Yeah people think everybody's luckier than they are. They think everyone on Instagram became successful overnight. Like success is a simple and easy to do. An effortless task that will only take a few days or weeks to achieve.

Okay. I'll have what their smoking!

But the truth is, you have to hustle and grind to get what you want in life. By the time I joined Instagram I was already successful. I also had a marketing budget for Facebook/Instagram. At the same time I started speaking at events which were marketed by other people as well as myself. So all of a sudden my ads and content were everywhere.

One of the key things I did was run local targeted ads just before the events to further enhance my exposure to my target market. This worked so well that I would go to other events weeks after the ones I spoke at and people would say they recognized me but they weren't sure how or from where.

They would often try to figure out if they knew me personally! As I explained briefly what they were experiencing, it would always lead to an extended conversation. And this is what I am sharing with you in this One Chapter Book.

This is a real – life conversation I had at an event. The names have been changed to protect the innocent. (I always wanted to say that)

In this chapter I share the 3 major mindset breakthroughs I had to allow me to become a LuckyPreneur. This will help you to see how you can achieve this for you and in your business too.

Thank you for joining me in this journey and being part of the One Chapter Book madness!

Dare to go where you mind leads you!

W.T.

Chapter 7.77 The LuckyPreneur : Does This Guy Have a Horseshoe up his Wazoo?

*E*verything I want to do, everything I focus on doing, and everything I believe I can do becomes the memories of my life.

I know, it's some heavy shit but it's the Real Real. This is the reality I live in. This is the kool-aid I'm drinking. This is the life I'm living.

This is what everyone sees from the outside. They see the Instagram life. The laptop lifestyle. They see the end result and then they wonder why I am so lucky? Why does everything work out for me? What's my story and how do I survive the entrepreneur struggle?

How do I know this? Because it almost always starts out in this way...

Random Stranger said to me, at a networking event, 'I see your face everywhere, you're doing so many things what's the deal? Do you have a horseshoe up your Wazoo?'

I instantly smiled at this brave and crazy MoFo. I smiled because this is evidence beyond any analytics that my marketing is working. (A little side note: If you want to get noticed you have to earn attention - You rarely get it for free)

So I replied to Random Stranger, 'LOL, everything is falling into place. I'm having a lot of fun and it's great to know that so many people are benefiting from what I'm doing.'

Random Stranger will often look kind of confused but the really bold MoFo's will persist. 'Tell me your secret, how are you everywhere and doing so many things? How are you doing it?'

They're always after my Lucky Charms - Paddy O'Brien from Austin Powers: International Man of Mystery.

So Random Stranger wanted to know my secret to being successful and I had no choice, I had to tell him because he asked and it's only the right thing to do. So I replied with a smile, 'I have a horseshoe up my Wazoo!'

Random Stranger laughed cause ya know, I'm a funny MoFo. But this answer wasn't going to be enough to satisfy Random Stranger, nope, he's the kind of guy that want answers and he'll stand awkwardly in front of you until he gets them. Unfortunately he looked like the kind of person that gathers vast amount of information but never actually uses any of it.

I decided to have some fun and phucwithhimforaminute just because I could.

So I said, 'Imagine if someone could have a horseshoe shoved up their ass. What would that conversation even look like? And who would you ask to do it? Your doctor?'...

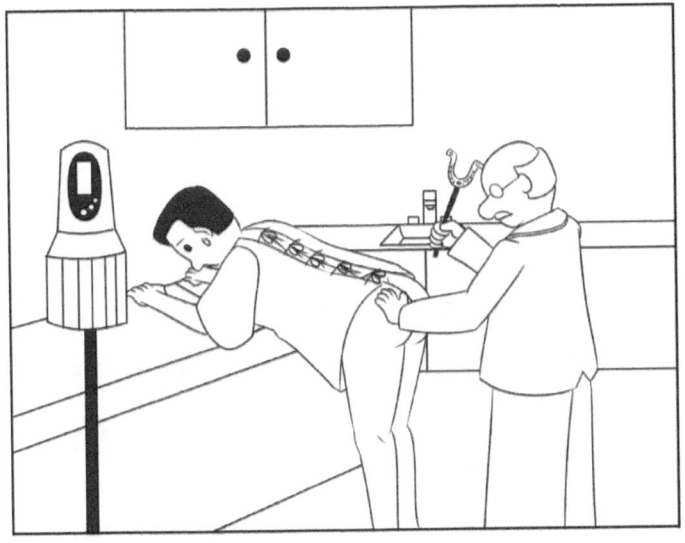

Imagine

Ok the fun was over. It was time to dazzle Random Stranger with my knowledge and insight on how he too could become a LuckyPreneur. One day I should create a One Chapter Book to help more people learn how to do this too. (Wait a minute, that's a great Idea...I'm on it!)

So I looked Random Stranger directly in the eyes and said, 'It's all about movement and momentum.' This was my Yoda shit, very intriguing.

'Movement and momentum?' Random Stranger was both confused and intrigued, just where I wanted him.

'The greatest plans, the most ambitious ideas and the clearest visions only become something from movement and momentum.' I said it with a friendly smile inviting him to dive deeper into this.

'But what is it you're doing to be able to have so many things happening at the same time. I mean I see you doing speaking engagements, releasing a bazillion books, taking selfies with important people at other events you're attending. Man you seem to be everywhere!'

What he was saying was all true.

I replied, 'I decided first on what I wanted to do, then I decided on what I was willing to do to get it. This is the first step in my process. This is how I create Luck in my business.'

'Ok' Random Stranger said, 'But what is the process, You gotta tell me how you're doing all these things so fast and making it look so easy?'

Now I'm not sure why Random Stranger felt like I owed him this insight but I really liked the MoFo's energy. I wanted to inspire him to really go for it and make his business take off so I decided to give him some free on the spot coaching. (My Mentor is going to kill me but it just felt like the right thing to do)

'I actually experienced 3 major mindset breakthroughs that allowed me to get out of my own way and really start magnetizing my goals and dreams.' I could see that Random Stranger couldn't wait to hear what I had to say next.

'The first breakthrough was the day I realized that nothing is as easy as it sounds or looks. Everything in life is a struggle. Relationships, jobs, MLM, Golf, it doesn't matter what it is, everything in life's a struggle until...' I paused for a moment to give it the dramatic effect needed to help Random Stranger really let the next part of what I was about to say sink in. It is something I've learned along the way. If the information doesn't sink into the subconscious it won't be retained. It has to have some impact and emotion to it to really stick.

'I learned how to do it, no matter what I was trying to do or how painful and frustrating it became because I discovered this. Once I learned how to do it, the thing I once struggled to do became easy. This was my first big breakthrough. Easy comes after the struggle to learn. The skill is in the struggle.' I paused for a quick moment as I watched his eyes begin to think about what I just said.

'Before this discovery I would start things with joy and excitement. I would count my money before I even made a dime! Thinking this one is the answer to all my problems, this is what I was looking for. But every time it became challenging, every time it got hard I would start to doubt I could do it. I would begin to think it's too difficult, it's a scam, it wasn't what I thought it would be and eventually I'd find the perfect excuse for why I couldn't do it anymore, so I could then feel good about quitting. Until... one day I suddenly realized, in life we have all been trained to make excuses for why we quit. It's our way of justifying failure and deferring the blame.

It wasn't my fault it didn't work, the MLM was too hard to sell. It wasn't my fault I didn't sell more, nobody wanted to buy my books. It wasn't my fault it didn't work, there are too many people already in this. And I found everyone around me spoke and thought the same way.

But what about the abundance of people that were successful doing the same thing I was quitting? How come they're so lucky? Do they have a horseshoe up their Wazoo?'

Random Stranger was so interested in what I was saying that he drew a few more listeners to our conversation. This was now turning into a speech.

'The answer was No! They didn't have any items of luck up their ass! What they had was the focus and drive to learn how to make it work. They knew the skill is in the challenge. The challenge creates the luck. So once I started to face the challenge I had no choice but to learn how to master it. And once I mastered it I owned that Bad Boy for the rest of my life. It didn't matter if I sold my business and started a new one or if I launched other streams of my business. Anytime I faced that challenge I now knew what it would take to overcome it. This was So Powerful for me. So I began to take easy off the table. Easy was no longer an option. That was the breakthrough that started the ball rolling.'

Just then, from the crowd, Pretty Eavesdropping Girl asked me, 'But how do you stay motivated when it seems like you're never gonna find the answer?'

I smiled, 'I wrote about this in my One Chapter Book - the Lonelypreneur - you have to build a team around you that understands what you are trying to do. You should really read that book to understand this concept in more detail. But here's something to think about. You have to ask yourself what skills, habits and attitudes do I need right now to get me to where I want to be? Because once you let go of easy, this opens up the door to the solution you need. You see when I wanted to start speaking on the main stage I didn't just decide I'd do that and then magically I start speaking on stage. That would be too easy and easy is not real so I had to start to investigate and gain a clear understanding of what people that speak on stage know. How did they develop their skills? How did they position themselves so they could get invited to speak on the main stage? And how did they market themselves?'

Pretty Eavesdropping Girl was now engaged in the conversation and became an active participant.

'You see, easy is a crutch. It holds no real value. It isn't very helpful and if you succeed at easy you'll never really learn how to build it again so you can repeat your success in the next venture.' This is one of my main lessons I teach beginners in how to become a LuckyPreneur.

Random Stranger didn't want to get left out of the talk so he ask, 'Ok, you said you had 3 major breakthroughs so what are the other two?'

I smiled as I began to giveaway another secret to my success. 'Well the second advancement took place when I decided to just be me.'

'When I first started learning about mindset and personal development I was introduced to the Law of Attraction. Each and every person that was talking about and using the Law of Attraction were a carbon copy of each other. They all talked the same way and believe the exact same things. But I felt fake trying to talk about it in this way and be like them. At the same time, I was building my entrepreneur consulting business and I was trying to imitate what I thought a business owner should sound like, look like and be like, but what I found was, I felt fake doing that too.'

I paused on purpose to allow them to relate as I knew everyone has this shared experience when jumping into something new.

I continued, 'I wasn't enjoying what I was doing or even who I was interacting with. I felt like I couldn't be me, until one day I said, *'PhucDis!'* And I just stopped being them and started being me. The very moment I did that I started to find my tribe. I began to connect with the people who were looking for what I was selling in the way I was selling it. Sure I lost some clients and support but I gained way more valuable clients and support by doing this because for the first time I was being the authentic me.'

Both Random Stranger and Pretty Eavesdropping Girl were smiling with joy. It was as if this was the first time someone had told them it's OK to be yourself.

Random Stranger then said, 'I love that. I feel like I spend more time trying to be what I think other people want me to be instead of just being me!'

'I know, it's so simple but we're afraid people won't like who we really are.' I replied.

Then Pretty Eavesdropping Girl added, 'This is my biggest fear. What if I put myself out there and nobodies like it? What if people start dissin me and I lose everything I built?'

Oh Snap! I found myself searching for a nice and compassionate way to answer this (Compassion and nice aren't always my strongest suit) I said, 'What if you become super successful being someone you're not? Would you really enjoy your success? Your life? If you become so popular and established that you could never be the real you again?'

'Holy shit!' She gasped, 'I never looked at it like that!'

'Most people don't, they look at the money and try to copy those around them that have already succeeded.' I then added, 'you can use someone else's blueprint but you need to put your own stank on it! Make it yours, customize that shit!'

At that moment another member in the crowd felt the need to add to the discussion. An impromptu talk like this always needs this guy to make it a memorable moment.

I Know Everything Guy piped up, 'You can't just tell people to forget about their branding and abandon their audience and act like its so easy dude, this is a bunch of horseshit!'

I had a genuinely ginormous smile on my face. 'Well you probably missed what I was saying earlier but I did say the first step is to take easy off the table. Of course your branding is very important. This is what you will use to attract your target audience. And your target is the kind of people you would love to work with every day. The people that will be inspired by you and will also inspire you. But you have to believe in what you are doing. If you don't believe that being the real you will work for you then it won't. So you also have to ask yourself one key thing, Are You Trading Your Happiness for Money?'

I Know Everything Guy was stumped for a moment. I could see it in his eyes. He was frantically searching for the next point to argue. He was racing against himself for something else to throw at me. It was his mission. 'So you're saying money's not important. Like you don't need money to run your business. What kind of crackpot advice is this?!?!' He wasn't smiling as he said that shit!

I hit him with a smile as I spoke, 'Money is not important. Profit is important. Your business needs to be making a profit to stay in business but how you make your money

IS important. Do you see the difference?' I already knew he wouldn't be able to make the clear distinction, I was just setting him up to give me permission to continue.

'Enlighten me smart guy.' I Know Everything Guy had a great personality for business. LOL!

I could see the rest of the audience was anxiously waiting for me to elaborate too.

'Whatever you do in life has to be profitable. You need to make money to feed your family, keep the lights on and to be able to help people, so making money is a given. You also need to know how much you need to make at any given time to be profitable and stay profitable. But the truth is, you can make money in many ways, honest ways, dishonest ways, being real, being fake, it doesn't matter. Money doesn't care how you make it but deep down you will never be happy if you're not living your passion. If you're not being the real you then you're trading your happiness for a buck. Money will never make you happy. It will make you comfortable. It will make things easier and you'll have some fun but once those fun moments pass all you have is money.'

I know Everything Guy thought he had an opening, 'I have a big house, nice cars, and I can do what I want so I'm happy. Who wouldn't be happy making lot of money? I'm very happy!'

'But are you? If your money train stops tomorrow would you still be happy?'

'Of course I would because I'd just go out and make more money!' I Know Everything Guy laughed loudly.

'But are you being the real you? Are you surrounded by people who are inspired to be around you or are you just surrounded by people who want something from you or who work for you?'

I Know Everything Guy didn't like this part of the conversation. I could see by the expression on his face, he was getting irritated.

I said, 'You probably work many hours calling it your hustle. You probably spend most of your time with clients, investors, acquaintances, and people who have a direct tie to your business and you call them your friends but are you only really having fun and satisfaction when you are spending your money or chasing money?'

At this point everyone in the conversation was looking at I Know Everything Guy waiting to hear his answer. I could see various emotions transform his face as the question swirled around and crashed against the walls of his cranium. I knew he didn't want to admit it but he knew the answer. He felt the answer and it was a punishingly humbling one to him.

I put my hand on his shoulder, 'I was there with you working for a company that only cared about the bottom line. There was no real heart, no real connection. So I put on my big boy pants and I left. I fired my boss and I found my passion. Was it scary? Hell Yeah! But it felt good. It felt right and I knew it would work out and become something great in the end. I decided to follow my passion. But the real turning point came when I let myself be authentic and real. That was the best decision I made. I became free from caring about what others thought and, the profits came to me even though I was no longer focused on the money.'

Pretty Eavesdropping Girl was moved and thanked me for sharing my truths with everyone. Suddenly she asked excitedly, 'So what was the 3rd big breakthrough you had?'

'Well the 3rd breakthrough was developing a crystal clear picture of what I wanted my success to look like.'

'How did you do that?' Pretty Eavesdropping Girl inquired.

'I started by defining my definition of success. What would success look like for me? What would success feel like for me? What would success sound like for me? What would success taste like for me?'

I looked everyone in the eyes as I said these words, even the extra few silent listeners that had gathered.

Random Stranger spoke, 'Success has a sound and taste? What is it a meal?'

Everyone laughed.

'It could be' I stated.

"It can be whatever you want it to be. Here's the trick. You need to make your success an exciting experience. Most people make it a thing like making X amount of money or buying a big house. Having a big office, getting an executive title. They're all things you get when you become successful but that's not really what success is. If you don't create a crystal clear definition of your success you could end up building someone else's definition of success and achieve those things but still not feeling fulfilled, satisfied or happy even though you may be rich!'

I could see the crowd wasn't very clear on what I was saying so I went deeper.

'My breakthrough came to me when I stopped looking at success as things I could have and started to look at it as experiences I wanted to…well…uno…experience!'

Everyone laughed as I continued, 'Your life is a series of experiences, good or bad. I realized if I focused on the experiences I wanted to have I would live them as long as I stayed focused on them for a long period of time.'

Now I could see the wheels turning. They were starting to get it.

'Let's say I wanted to sell lots of books. The first thing I would do is write down what that experience would feel like. Where would I be when I got the news? Who would I tell first? What would I do next? The more I started to focus on it the more details I could add to the picture I was creating in my mind of this event. Then I began to see that if I made a reward for myself attached with the achievement, once I hit that goal I could measure if I had the success I wanted or if I was experiencing something close to it but not the full success I was looking for.'

I Know Everything Guy piped up, 'But why did you say lots of books instead of saying millions of books? Wouldn't it be better to be more specific?'

I smiled happily, 'And that's where the breakthrough led me. When you really get focused on the goal you will start to make big confident and sometimes scary goals like saying I want to sell millions of books. The more focused and clear you can get the greater your chance gets to experience that goal. But here's the real challenge, you have to learn how to build the experience in your mind like a memory you've already lived!'

I watched as the smiles grew on each person's face. They quickly began to see in their mind all the possibilities they had in front of them. They could see all the ways they could change their lives just by learning how to do this. I looked at Random Stranger.

'Look what you've started all from one simple question.' I could see that he almost forgot this all began when he asked if I had a horseshoe up my Wazoo.

'Yeah, so this is how you do it huh?!?' He was thinking as he spoke.

'With these key breakthroughs I was able to create one of the most important things needed to become a LuckyPreneur and that is movement & momentum.'

'Can't wait to hear this one!' I Know Everything Guy said sarcastically as he rolled his eyes.

I looked directly at him as I unleashed this knowledge storm, 'Once I knew who I was, had a crystal clear vision of what my success looked like and I took easy off the table I was ready to start making a plan. I was ready to do what it took to bring the results in that I wanted.'

What is Luck?

'I knew there's not just one way to sell my books but many ways. I knew I needed to engage with people. Market myself and my books. Be where my audience is and show my audience my success so they will be inspired to learn from me.'

I Know Everything Guy interrupted me, 'Yeah that all sounds great but how is that going to help me?'

I really love this guy. 'It's called getting out of your own way. I knew I had to do the hard things like talking about myself or my books online and offline day after day even when I felt like it was too much. I had to set things into motion and then learn how to step away from the result. Let it grow how it will grow. And the more I did this the more I had people come up to me like tonight saying 'Do you have a horseshoe up your Ass?' That's how you become a LuckyPreneur.'

'So it's all about marketing. Anyone can do that!' I Know Everything Guy didn't seem to know too much. (He probably needs a new name)

'No, it's not really marketing. It's about the hustle and grind. Knowing when to hustle and when to sit back and let your hustle work for you. It's engaging and attracting people to what you do. You have to be real with people. Have real conversations online and offline. You have to be willing to create the luck in your business.'

I looked at each person that was gathered around me and I asked this question.

'What is Luck?'

A world wind of thought blasted everyone. Then I Know Everything Guy gave me the opening I was waiting for. It's the classic answer to the question.

He said. 'It's being in the right place at the right time.'

'And how do you get into the right place at the right time?' I asked.

'It's all about who you know!' He said a matter-of- factly.

'But how do you get to know those important people?' I pushed.

'Luck?' He didn't know what else to say.

'Luck is the result of creating opportunities that you're prepared to take advantage of.' This was the deep insight I usually charge big bucks for.

'The key to being a LuckyPreneur is to create many opportunities in multiple areas and being ready to say Yes when that opportunity manifest. But it can only be created by movement and momentum.' I paused.

'Every connection I made was because I did something on purpose first. Attending an event, posting a blog or video, engaging on and off line or simply making myself standout.'

I had given them a lot to think about in just this one conversation but I felt I needed to wrap it up in a way that would leave them inspired and motivated to pursue being a LuckyPreneur.

'My secret to achieving this was the moment the hustle and grind no longer felt like a hustle and grind. It was the moment I fell in love with my business. The moment when what I was doing became fun. This was a game changer for me. This opened the doors to luck and aligned me with what I wanted to succeed at.'

Each person had a look of imagination on their faces; dreaming of turning their hustle and grind into their definition of fun & success in this way.

'And it all started for me from achieving the 3 breakthroughs I talked about which led me to many other breakthroughs as I learned, expanded and grew.'

I Know Everything Guy smiled, 'I like that! I knew the answer already but I wanted to test you.' He laughed but as he did Pretty Eavesdropping Girl said, 'Yeah right!' Then everyone laughed.

Random Stranger then said, 'So you really developed a routine and system to help you build your success and with hard work, thought out goals and some drive you were able to make it look easy!' He felt proud to have figured out my secret trick.

'Yes, sometimes the simplest solution looks too simple so people bypass it for something more difficult. The key is to really know what you want to do and stick to it until people think you have a horseshoe up your Wazoo! This is how you become a LuckyPreneur. You become one on purpose.'

I could see that people wanted to go deeper into this but this impromptu training session needed to come to a close so I said to everyone, 'I'd love to help you further and see you really accelerate your success so if you can take out your smartphones and go to https://www.instagram.com/w.t.hamilton/ and DM me with your questions and I will be more than happy to assist you in any way I can and guide you to my books and programs that will really help you accelerate your success!'

They all thanked me for taking the time to entertain them with my knowledge and insight. After some closing chit chats, one by one each person walked away until it was just me and I Know Everything Guy left.

'Can I ask you something?' He said.

'Sure what is it?' I was prepared for anything at this point.

'Would you coach me?' He said sheepishly.

I shook my head up and down and smiled. 'Do you know what you're getting into?' I asked. (Yes I was asking him but I really was asking myself.)
He simply said 'Yes' and our journey was about to begin.

Final Thoughts

Many entrepreneurs get lost in the hustle and grind. Too many coaches and mentors push the idea that you have to be doing something all the time to create success. But the truth is luck is about giving luck more ways to find you. Throughout this chapter I've given you nuggets, tool & techniques to show you how to create luck in your business.

By following the lessons within the story you will have a great start to creating your best business environment for success. As you may have discovered, your mindset is a significant part of your success. With the right mindset you can get out of your own way and let luck enter your life.

This story was written to help you really understand just how powerful you can be with the right attitude toward what you are doing. Throughout life we are taught to invest in marketing, content development, formal education, money growth strategies but never about investing in your own personal growth and development. But without the right mindset all of these things will never reach their full potential. Only you can drive the goal to its fullest reality by believing you can and you must.

Read this book again and take notes. Write down the key lessons and think about how you can apply this to your business. Look at where you are right now and what you could change to create the new YOU – the LuckyPreneur YOU.

Thank you for joining me on this journey of success.

Until Next Time...

W.T. Hamilton

Visit us at www.wherethewindblows.ca

Follow Me on Social Media

https://twitter.com/w_t_hamilton

https://itunes.apple.com/ca/podcast/w-t-hamilton/id1364289273

https://www.youtube.com/channel/UC4W6Oy1jb7U64B0U9uzGadA

https://www.instagram.com/w.t.hamilton/

Get Our Your Invincible Power Motivational Book Series and More One Chapter Book Titles here:

https://www.amazon.com/W.-T.-Hamilton/e/B00YY0S4KK

Copyright © 2018 Your Invincible Power

All rights reserved

Published by W.T. Hamilton

Big Ups

Big ups to my Mom for working with me in this book and empowerment business. And for always supporting me in the many adventures of life.

Big up to my Dad for the encouragement, love and support throughout every step and also for teaching me how to be a Dad.

Big up to my kids for keeping me young at heart and always giving me reasons to laugh, feel proud and drink!

Big up to Fanny Newport (my Ride or Die) for loving me as I am and putting up with my crazy life and letting me not grow up.

To all my extended family who are always throwing love my way. Beers & BBQ's for life!!!

To my many friends old and new – I'm always thinking about how lucky I am to have people that come into my life for short or long term that make my life better than it would have been if I never met you. You guys and girls get a virtual high five!!!

And to you, Yeah the reader, I give you a special Big Up for investing time and money into you. For the hunger to make a positive change in your life and make your life the best it can be. Keep doing what you're doing. Keep reaching for the top. You got this!!!

You did it! You read the whole book!

You should give yourself a reward.

As a matter of fact, you should always give yourself a reward every time you complete something in self-improvement.

Think of something that will e very rewarding to treat yourself too.

It could be something small or something big but make sure you do something special for yourself, you've earned it.

That's the END

There's nothing
more to read.

It's Time to DO

Go Make It Happen!

Seriously

Go MoFo

It's Your Time Now!

Really?

You want more?

'This is definitely breaking the rules of publishing and writing for that matter so of course I'll give you a little more. You're ambitious and I like that.' I know Everything Guy thought it was strange that I spoke to him as if he was a character in my new book.

'One of my big breakthrough strategies was the day I decided to attend an event by myself.' I stated with a slight smile.

'I went to an event I was very interested in but either no one could attend with me or they weren't interested so I had two choices, Go by myself or don't go at all!' (Because of the earlier statement that this is a big breakthrough strategy I think it's Capt'n Obvious which one I went with!)

'This forced me to step way out of my comfort zone and start engaging with people. I had to walk up to groups, individuals and some intimidating looking people or sit in the corner talking to myself.' I Know Everything Guy smiled as he pictured me siting in a corner, holding a beer, with a sad look on my face while talking to myself. That heartless bastard!

'But as I approached people it was like that we're happy I came up to them. They were curious about me. Why I was there by myself? Why was I so confident? What do I do? What do I know?' As I spoke I Know Everything Guy leaned in a little as if what I was saying was going to be more powerful if his ears got closer to my mouth!?!?

'The result of this was, I stood out. People noticed me and wanted to engage. This was movement in action. It was from that experience that I began to understand the power of movement.' He was liking what I was saying. It spoke to his own struggles with interacting at events.

'From that I created a plan. It was a simple plan but this plan really brought great results. Its two steps in creating luck. First, I always try to get a selfie pic with the event host and people that seem to attract a crowd. Second, I always focus on being comfortable being uncomfortable.' I let that last part sink in a bit before I continued.

'I knew the more I got out of my comfort zone the less limits I had in everything I do. Once I got comfortable taking risks in this way I rapidly attracted huge amount of luck into my business and personal life.'

I Know Everything Guy was living this strategy, 'I'm glad I stuck around, this rocks. But how did you get out of your comfort zone? I mean, it's easy to say but doing it is a whole other story.' He said laughingly.

'One step at a time.' I smiled.

'You just have to make even the smallest of efforts toward something that breaks you out of you comfort zone.' I know this sounds simpler than it is.

'The reason people get hung up on it or get stuck is, they are trying to control the outcome. They have too much invested in the result. But the result is not important. And the harsh truth is, if it's your first time stepping out of your comfort zone it may not be as awesome as you think it will be but...'

I took a breath.

'You will feel a thrill once you've done it. You will also realize you're still alive and no one was laughing at you. You stepped out of your comfort zone and you didn't die. That is the best result & reward and can only lead to bigger things as you grow in your new comfort.'

I know Everything Guy's mind was building future possibilities as we spoke. I could see his excitement in his eyes.

'There are many mindset breakthroughs I will share with you and some awesome strategies too. This is just the beginning.' I wanted to reassure him and let I Know Everything Guy know that he didn't have to learn it all tonight.

'I will show you how to make this strategy into a game so you can measure your results and set targets for events and interactions. This is more than just a cool way to get out of your comfort zone. I'm gonna teach you how to use it for you marketing too. I will show you how even using this one result can turn you into the LuckPreneur.'

I Know Everything Guy couldn't wait to learn it and I could wait to teach him it. My Powerful Business Breakthroughs and Awesome Breakthrough Strategies to help You Stand Out and Get Paid.

That probably won't be the title when I write it. I'll probably call it something crazy that will make you actually want to see what the book is all about. Yeah that's what I'll do. That's the authentic me. Just the way I like it!

www.ingramcontent.com/pod-product-compliance
Lightning Source LLC
Chambersburg PA
CBHW031544210526
45464CB00003B/1144